FLOODWATERS AND FLAMES

THE 1913 DISASTER IN DAYTON, OHIO

LOIS MINER HUEY

M Millbrook Press/Minneapolis

For my beloved sister, Marion Miner Quiram

I wish to thank the wonderful people at the Dayton Metro Library and the Miami Conservancy District office for their help with this project, and special thanks to Curt Dalton for making his research available online. I also am thankful for the input on these stories by my critique groups and by editors Carol Hinz and Jenny Krueger, who made it so much better. —L.M.H.

Millbrook Press
A division of Lerner Publishing Group, Inc.
241 First Avenue North
Minneapolis, MN 55401 USA

For reading levels and more information, look up this title at www.lernerbooks.com.

Main body text set in Adobe Garamond Pro Regular 15/18.
Typeface provided by Adobe Systems.

Library of Congress Cataloging-in-Publication Data

Names: Huey, Lois Miner.
Title: Floodwaters and flames : the 1913 disaster in Dayton, Ohio / Lois Miner Huey.
Description: Minneapolis : Millbrook Press, 2016. | Audience: Grades 4 to 6. | Includes bibliographical references and index.
Identifiers: LCCN 2015018889| ISBN 9781467794329 (library bound : alkaline paper) | ISBN 9781467797283 (PDF)
Subjects: LCSH: Dayton (Ohio)—History—20th century—Juvenile literature. | Floods—Ohio—Dayton—History—20th century—Juvenile literature. | Fires—Ohio—Dayton—History—20th century—Juvenile literature. | Disaster victims—Ohio—Dayton—Biography—Juvenile literature. | Dayton (Ohio)—Biography—Juvenile literature.
Classification: LCC F499.D2 H84 2016 | DDC 977.1/73—dc23
LC record available at http://lccn.loc.gov/2015018889

Manufactured in the United States of America
1 – DP – 12/31/15

CONTENTS

Downtown Dayton, Ohio, in the early twentieth century

INTRODUCTION

DAYTON, OHIO, SPRING 1913

Coal dealer Andrew Fox looked out his window on the night of Monday, March 24. He could hear the wind howl, as it had for days. Hurricane-force winds of 70 to 90 miles (113 to 145 kilometers) per hour had roared into Dayton on Thursday and Friday. Telephone and telegraph poles had crashed to the ground. An ice storm followed. By Saturday most of the telephone wires were downed by ice. The rain beat down that Easter Sunday and into Monday.

"Received meager reports . . . that the Miami
River . . . was rising rapidly. Certainly no general
flood is expected."

—Dayton telegraph operator, log entry for 4 a.m. March 25

His neighbors called him "High Water" Fox. For years, he had warned of a
possible flood. Each time he sounded the alarm, his neighbors scrambled to higher
ground. Each time it was for nothing. To the residents of Dayton, Ohio, Fox was
like the fabled Boy Who Cried Wolf. But Fox was especially worried this time.
He knew the ground was already saturated from the snowmelt that spring. And it
didn't look as though the rain was going to let up anytime soon.

The city of Dayton was built where three tributaries of the Great Miami River
meet—the Stillwater River, the Mad River, and Wolf Creek. Fox worried that
the rivers could overflow into the city. Dayton was surrounded by hills. If people
could get to higher ground, they would be safe. But they would need time and
warnings. Downtown Dayton was supposed to be protected from flood by 20-foot-
high (6-meter) levees, built and rebuilt after several previous floods in the early
nineteenth century. Most people in town thought the levees would protect them,
so they weren't worried about the threat of flooding. But Fox was.

He grabbed his lantern and ran through the rain from his home on North
Main Street to the Herman Street levee. He peered at the height of the water
against the earthen walls. The water was only a few feet away from the top.

Fox ran through the streets, knocking on his neighbors' doors and yelling all
the way. This was the big one, the flood he'd feared all these years. His neighbors
either ignored him or laughed and shut their doors. He tried calling the police
department. It was now four o'clock in the morning, and the police also ignored
Fox's warning. Later that morning, Fox and his wife, Finette, packed their
belongings. They loaded what they could into his coal wagon and headed for
higher ground.

WATER RUSHES IN

At around 8:10 on Tuesday morning, water from the Great Miami River and its tributaries rushed into the city at a speed of 25 miles (40 km) per hour. Church bells rang and factory whistles blew, sounding their desperate warnings. Frantic people in the flood's path climbed trees. A witness recalled, "One great tree with spreading boughs was so thickly populated with women and children in various colored clothing that it looked like some great Christmas tree hung with huge dolls."

Others scaled telephone poles to save themselves. Those in buildings ran to upper floors and rooftops. The scene below was horrifying—horses swimming for their lives, heads held high. Streetcars overturned, spilling out passengers. Houses swept up in the water rushed past with people clinging to their porches.

The amount of water that rushed into Dayton was about equal to four days of water flow over Niagara Falls.

Survivors attempt to travel to safety by walking from pole to pole across telegraph wires.

"High Water" Fox had been right. The levees could not hold the water. The Great Miami River did the most damage, spilling into the heart of the city. The flood covered more than 14 square miles (36 sq. km) of land.

The coming chapters tell the stories of residents who were caught in the Great Dayton Flood of 1913. Some of these people, such as Orville Wright and John Patterson, were famous or powerful. Others, such as Bill Sloan, Mary Althoff, and Clarence Mauch, were ordinary citizens who became known for the roles they played during the flood. The story follows the lives of these key residents during three days of the disaster—Tuesday, Wednesday, and Thursday.

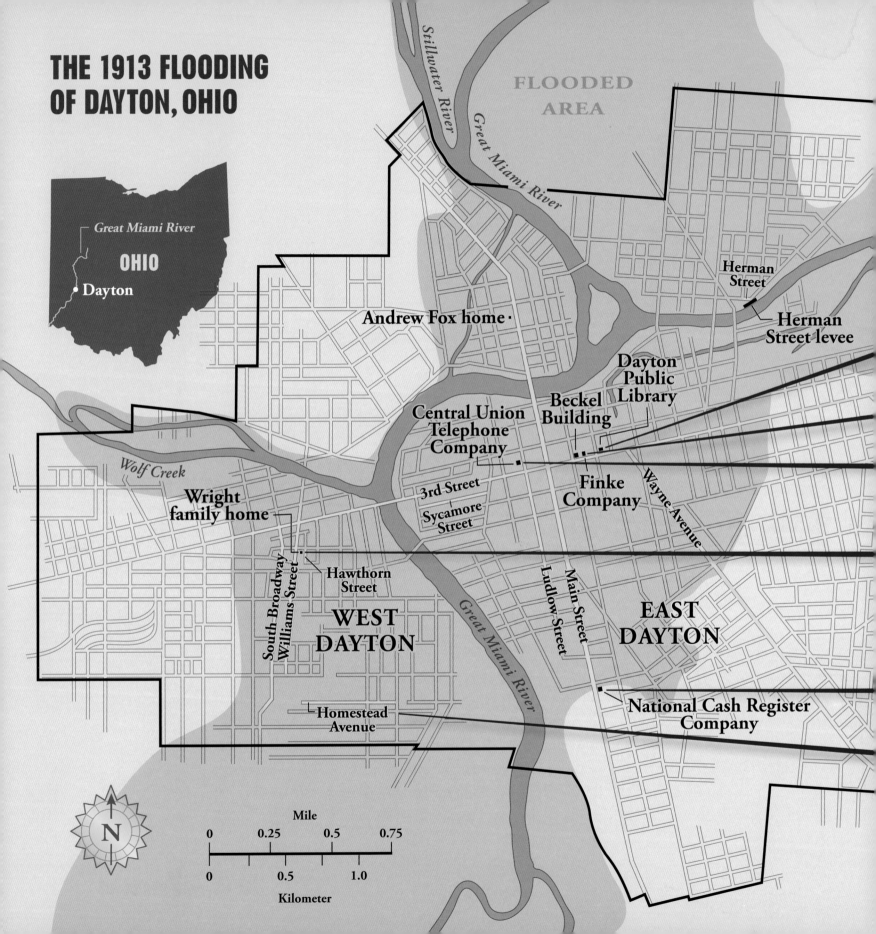

THE 1913 FLOODING OF DAYTON, OHIO

Great Miami River

OHIO

• Dayton

FLOODED AREA

Stillwater River

Great Miami River

Herman Street

Herman Street levee

Andrew Fox home ·

Dayton Public Library

Beckel Building

Central Union Telephone Company

Wolf Creek

Wright family home

3rd Street

Sycamore Street

Finke Company

Wayne Avenue

South Broadway Williams Street

Hawthorn Street

WEST DAYTON

Main Street Ludlow Street

EAST DAYTON

Great Miami River

Homestead Avenue

National Cash Register Company

N

Mile

0   0.25   0.5   0.75

0   0.5   1.0

Kilometer

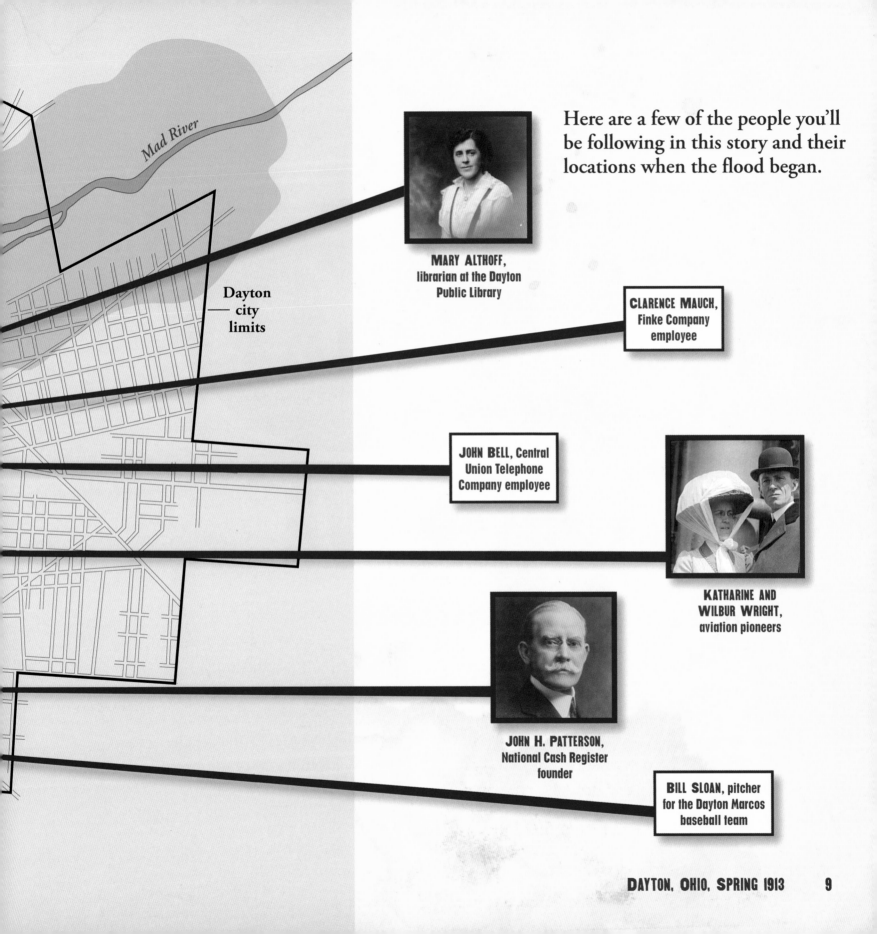

Here are a few of the people you'll be following in this story and their locations when the flood began.

MARY ALTHOFF, librarian at the Dayton Public Library

CLARENCE MAUCH, Finke Company employee

JOHN BELL, Central Union Telephone Company employee

KATHARINE AND WILBUR WRIGHT, aviation pioneers

JOHN H. PATTERSON, National Cash Register founder

BILL SLOAN, pitcher for the Dayton Marcos baseball team

Mad River

Dayton — city limits

John H. Patterson

CHAPTER ONE

A TIDAL WAVE

TUESDAY MORNING, MARCH 25

By eight o'clock on Tuesday morning, residents from all parts of Dayton were headed to work downtown. Despite the ongoing storms, most people thought Tuesday would be like any other ordinary day. The streets and sidewalks were full of people. They carried umbrellas and dodged puddles. They rode streetcars to businesses while men on horses threaded their way through traffic. As the people hustled to work or ran errands, the waters rose ever closer to the tops of the levees that were supposed to protect the city.

JOHN PATTERSON

John Patterson arrived at the factory of the National Cash Register Company at six thirty Tuesday morning. At the age of sixty-nine, Patterson had plenty of energy, and his business was thriving. The National Cash Register Company employed seven thousand people working in fifteen buildings on the hills above Dayton. Patterson gave workers extras such as day care for their children, dorms for those who worked long hours, and cafeterias. The National Cash Register Company was like a city within Dayton.

When Patterson reached his office, he immediately looked out a window at the water rising in the rivers below. Patterson had lived in Dayton his whole life. He knew that a flood in a city surrounded by rivers could mean disaster. His factory on the hills would be an ideal place to prepare for rescues, should they be needed. He quickly called his staff together and issued orders. His workers jumped to follow his instructions. The cooks in the kitchen were to make two thousand loaves of bread and 500 gallons (1,893 liters) of soup. Other employees gathered cots, beds, blankets, pillows, clothing, and shoes of all sizes. Even as they worked, waters began to spill over the tops of the levees.

The typewriting department at the National Cash Register Company

Patterson had his 150 carpenters start making flat-bottomed rescue boats large enough to hold six people each. The men usually built shipping crates. They had never made boats before. But these skilled carpenters began turning out one boat every seventeen minutes for a total of almost three hundred. Patterson ordered his men to take the boats closer to downtown to get ready for rescues. By noon the first boats set out, but the rushing water made rescues impossible.

Back at the factory, employees hurried to set up cots, medicines from the company's infirmary, and extra chairs and tables in the cafeteria. On Patterson's orders, they quietly prepared some of the cooler rooms to create a makeshift morgue to hold dead bodies.

THE 1913 STORM SYSTEM

The weather that caused the 1913 flood began west of Dayton. The storm system swept east across the Midwest to the East Coast. Nebraska, Indiana, Tennessee, and New York were some of the hardest-hit states.

Patterson had his employees organize a soup kitchen to feed stranded flood survivors.

JOHN BELL

Telephone company manager John Bell arrived at his downtown office after a short walk through the driving rain. When water began to wash into the building, Bell and his employees knew they were facing an emergency. They had to work fast to save telephone service to the outside world.

Bell grabbed a phone and went to the roof where he could get a better picture of what was happening. He was able to connect the phone to a surviving telephone line that went to a town called Phoneton, Ohio. This was the hub of telephone communication at the time. He knew reaching Phoneton would be his best chance to connect to another phone network. It worked. An operator in Phoneton forwarded Bell's call through to Columbus, the state capital. Over and over, Bell tried to call Ohio governor James M. Cox. Bell had to tell the outside world that Dayton needed help.

Bell used a crank-operated phone to call Governor Cox. Bell and his employees hauled a large battery to the roof that could power the phone so that he would not have to turn the crank through the night.

ORVILLE AND KATHARINE WRIGHT

Forty-two-year-old Orville Wright lived on Hawthorn Street with his sister, Katharine, and their father, Bishop Milton Wright. In 1903 Orville had piloted an aircraft he had designed with his brother, Wilbur, for the first controlled airplane flight in history. After Wilbur died in 1912, Orville traveled the world with Katharine to sell airplanes. They had recently come home for Easter.

On Tuesday morning, eighty-four-year-old Bishop Wright watched out the window as the waters burst onto their street. He saw a canoe approach his window.

Orville and Katharine Wright pictured at the family home that was being built at the time of the flood. They moved from their much smaller house on Hawthorn Street after the flood.

Orville and Katharine Wright were successful business partners. Orville, an inventor, was shy and reserved. He left the selling of their products to Katharine, who was outgoing and social.

The paddlers offered to take Bishop Wright with them to higher ground. His son and daughter urged him to go. One of the boaters carried the Bishop on his shoulders to the boat. They didn't know where they were going, but they knew they had to escape the rising waters.

Orville and Katharine Wright watched their father climb in, and the canoe disappeared down the street. Katharine adjusted her wire-rimmed glasses and smoothed the dark hair pulled back behind her head. They would stay to protect the house. The factory where their airplanes were built was on a hill overlooking Dayton, so they knew that would be safe.

Katharine and Orville rushed to move furniture and books to the second floor. As the water rose outside, they realized they couldn't stay. They saw neighbors in a horse and buggy struggling through the water. The neighbors invited the Wrights to join them. The Wrights climbed in, realizing how serious this flood really was. They worried about their father. Had he made it to safety?

CLARENCE MAUCH

Eighteen-year-old Clarence Mauch walked to his job as a store clerk at the Finke Company on East Third Street. The company sold school supplies and other items to local stores. "I had no difficulty," Mauch remembered, "until Wayne Avenue." There he had to wade through water almost up to his knees.

When Mauch arrived at the three-story brick building, he found his boss and two other men in the basement. They were already packing load after load of merchandise onto a rope-operated elevator. Mauch ran to pull the rope and haul goods to the third floor. There they stacked the goods on shelves. They then began hauling merchandise up from the first floor.

By a quarter past eight, the basement was completely flooded and water was rising onto the first floor. The men worked faster. On the upper floor, they threw goods out of the elevator, no longer carefully stacking them. A loud boom sent them rushing to a window. Flames had burst from a building nearby. They knew they had to abandon the Finke Company store before it too caught on fire.

Floodwaters rise toward the second story of houses on Sycamore Street.

SYCAMORE ST.   68.

Grabbing books and records, Mauch and the others pushed out the door and waded through water almost waist-high. They struggled to walk as the surging water rose nearly to their chests. They came to the Beckel Building, which stood 4 feet (1 m) above street level. Grateful for this dry spot, they climbed the steps to safety. Nine

GAS LINES

Natural gas is delivered through pipes into buildings and houses. It is used for cooking and heating and, in 1913, for lighting. At that time, the pipes to deliver gas were metal. Today plastic pipes are used to lower the risk of metal causing a spark and igniting gas fumes. Since the 1930s, an odor has been added to natural gas so those nearby can smell a leak and leave the area. That was not practiced in 1913, however. The people of Dayton could not have smelled the leaking gas, so they had no warning before explosions.

others were already in the building, which housed a bank. A bank official kindly put the Finke Company books and records in the bank safe.

Within minutes, the water had risen inside the building almost to their knees. More people crowded in, and two horses swimming by climbed the steps to join them. Outside the door, the water was 6 feet (1.8 m) deep, over many of their heads. They were trapped with water rising all around them. Leaning out an upper-floor window, one of them saw a long wooden sign that read TYPEWRITERS on the outside wall of the building. A few men jumped onto the windowsill and tugged until the sign ripped away into their hands.

The sign was 12 feet (4 m) long and 18 inches (46 centimeters) wide. They pulled it inside and used leather straps taken from the horses to anchor it to a heavy desk. They pushed the sign out a window so that it landed on the windowsill of a building only a few feet north and on slightly higher ground. "One by one, we crawled on the plank," Mauch said. The horses had to be left behind.

By noon they had all made it to the next building. They were "happy to reach this dry haven," Mauch remembered. Other men and women already in

Floodwaters nearly reach the tops of streetlights on Ludlow Street.

the building greeted them. Altogether, there were twenty-five to thirty people in the building. It was close enough to its neighbors that some of the group made a successful trip across roofs and through upper windows into a grocery store. They were able to bring back canned meats, cheeses, and crackers. An employee of the grocery store made a list of the items, expecting payment later.

As the afternoon wore on, the temperature dropped. There was no heat in the building. Mauch and his companions shivered and huddled together.

The library building at Third and Patterson Streets

MARY ALTHOFF

When librarian Mary Althoff reached the Dayton Public Library on Tuesday morning, water was already creeping toward the building. Althoff gathered her long skirts and hurried up the steps. The library basement held children's books, documents, newspapers, and supplies. She thought she'd better get those paper goods onto higher shelves, just in case.

She found janitor Edward Harvey already inside the building. She later wrote that the two discussed "the possibility of a break in the levees—though scarcely dreaming that such a thing could really happen."

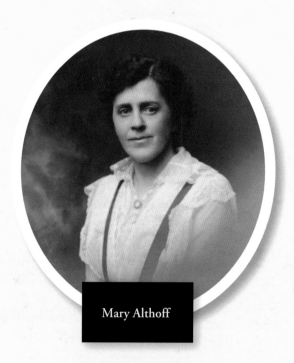

Mary Althoff

To be safe, though, they began stacking as many of the twenty thousand volumes of children's books, newspapers, and special collection items as they could onto the top shelves in the basement. Their arms ached, but they kept at it.

Water began gushing through the stone foundation, pouring into the basement. Althoff turned toward the stairs, "when suddenly there was a terrific noise; the east doors and windows were thrown violently open and a great surge of black muddy water rushed in like a tidal wave upon us." She screamed a warning to Harvey and dashed up to the main floor. Althoff later reported that the janitor was "caught in the waves to his waist, and only with the greatest difficulty succeeded in reaching the first floor."

Books in the basement of the Dayton Public Library were damaged or destroyed when floodwaters poured through the building's foundation.

BILL SLOAN

Bill Sloan lived on the west side of Dayton, across the Great Miami River from downtown. He waved to friends as he walked toward his job at the Kuhns Brothers Foundry a few blocks from his house on Homestead Avenue. Sloan was a well-known pitcher for the local Dayton Marcos baseball team. In the off-season, he worked as a laborer at a foundry. Sloan's neighborhood was a mix of white and African American residents, mostly laborers, craftsmen, and their families.

Sloan was alarmed when he heard the church bells and factory whistles sound across the Great Miami River. When he was eight years old, he had experienced the flood of 1898, the last major flood to hit the area. He knew that the heavy rains and alarms likely meant another flood was on the way.

Thinking quickly, Sloan remembered that the manager of the Dayton D Handle Company had a good steel-bottomed boat and that the company was only a couple of blocks away. Sloan rushed across the railroad tracks, heading for South Broadway.

The Dayton Marcos baseball team, circa 1920

Dayton's poorer neighborhoods were crowded with families living in homes that were easily swept away in the floodwaters.

He ran up the stairs to the office of the manager, Leroy Crandall. Crandall too had heard the alarms, but he was sitting at his desk, apparently not worried.

Sloan told Crandall his plan. He needed to borrow the rowboat—and fast. Crandall refused and went back to his work. Sloan clenched a fist—he was certain there were people who needed his help. He eventually threatened Crandall with a handgun. Crandall backed down and finally agreed to let Sloan use the boat. Sloan ran down the stairs to the back of the building. Two men nearby helped him carry the boat back toward his neighborhood.

By then water was swiftly running down the streets of the west side of Dayton. Sloan put the rowboat into the current and began paddling. He had strong arms from working in the foundry and from baseball, and he would need them. His work had just begun.

MARY ALTHOFF

Standing on the stairs above the first floor of the library, Mary Althoff and Edward Harvey watched in horror as the water rose and spread across the main floor. Bookcases fell, dropping books into the water. Desks, tables, chairs, and files floated around like bath toys. Glass doors on cabinets shattered. "The black waters swirled around the building with a deafening roar. How was all this going to end?" she wondered.

Shaking from exhaustion and shocked at what they'd seen, Althoff and Harvey went to the second floor, where the town's museum was housed. Althoff looked around at the dozens of glass cases that held fossils, mounted insects, and historic items. On the wall hung stuffed eagles with outstretched wings; a Native American canoe; and the hides of a zebra, leopard, and buffalo. Would all these treasures be lost too?

Seven men and a woman were already there, clustered at a window. Althoff and Harvey joined them to see the nightmare below. Rain poured down. Houses, porches, automobiles, carriages,

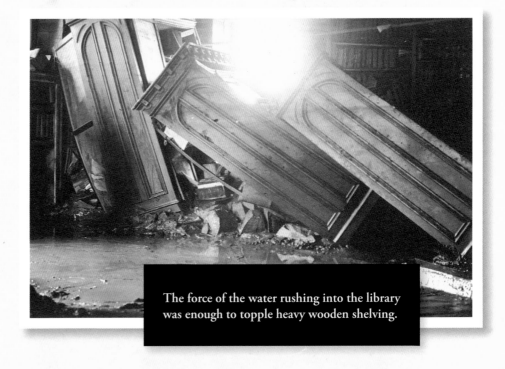

The force of the water rushing into the library was enough to topple heavy wooden shelving.

and horses rushed by, carried by the floodwater. Althoff wondered about the safety of her family—her brother and parents. She had lived in Dayton all her forty-four years. She had never seen anything like this.

Horses swim in water rushing down Fourth Street.

Around a corner came a young man on a horse, caught up in the surging water. The boy tried to steer the horse toward the library, but the panicked animal kept swimming. It became wedged in a large elm tree across the flooded street. The horse struggled to free itself. The boy pulled himself onto a branch as the water climbed higher and higher. When he unfastened the reins, the horse thrashed free and swam away. Climbing to a higher branch, the boy tied himself to the tree trunk with the reins. He called for help over and over. Althoff and the others could do nothing.

"Perhaps the queerest sight of all was a table we saw floating by us. It was set for dinner. Plates were laid for four, and in the center was a catsup bottle and a sugar bowl, with a menu card between."

—*Richard Filley, railroad conductor*

JOHN BELL

On Tuesday afternoon, Bell finally reached Governor Cox's office in Columbus. Over his one precious wire to the outside world, Bell told the governor what he saw: People, horses, and debris caught in the rushing water. People were jumping off roofs to escape fires. The governor was shocked. Heavy rain was falling in Columbus too, with some flooding, but nothing like what was happening in Dayton. Bell continued reporting to the governor off and on through Tuesday night. Cox promised to see what he could do and said he would get back to Bell when he had some news.

BILL SLOAN

Bill Sloan rowed victims to higher ground all day Tuesday and into Tuesday night. The survivors were grateful for Sloan's rescue and for a drink from the 5 gallons (19 liters) of fresh water he carried with him. The west side of Dayton was completely flooded, including the building that housed the Dayton D Handle Company. Among the many people Sloan rescued that night was the manager whose boat he had taken, Leroy Crandall.

ORVILLE AND KATHARINE WRIGHT

Orville and Katharine Wright had taken shelter out of the flood zone with a friend. They worried about their father. They had no way of contacting or finding him. Had the canoe turned over? Was he somewhere safe? They went to bed hoping the next day would bring an end to this nightmare.

MARY ALTHOFF

No one slept well at the library Tuesday night. Every fifteen minutes, Althoff and the others took turns leaning out the windows to call to the boy in the tree. They shouted, "All right? Hang on!" Sometimes the boy would answer, but Althoff reported that his voice was "so faint we could scarcely hear."

CLARENCE MAUCH

Back at the Beckel Building, Clarence Mauch and his companions continued to huddle in the cold. Mauch later described the "dark hours of a long, dreary night" with all "deeply concerned for the welfare of our families and homes, now in the flooded and darkened city. Yes, it was a night to be long remembered."

ANDREW FOX

"High Water" Fox and his wife sat on his horse-drawn coal wagon on a hill above the city for most of the day. Finette Fox held an umbrella over her head and cried as she watched water rush into their neighborhood. They were safe, but they saw their neighbors scrambling onto the roofs of their homes, desperate to escape.

That night was the darkest night the Foxes and the other people of Dayton had ever experienced. There were no lanterns or streetlights. Black clouds masked the moon. The rain had changed to snow and sleet. Temperatures fell to 3°F (–16°C). The Foxes slept fitfully inside the coal wagon as floodwaters continued to roar.

An illustration dated March 26, 1913, shows the flames that lit up Dayton through the night.

BIRDS-EYE VIEW OF THE BUSINESS SECTION OF DAYTON, OHIO. SKETCHED MARCH 26, 1913. LOOKING EAST FROM WILLIAMS ST.
Now Being Rebuilt with Greater Rapidity and Vigor Than Any Other Calamity in the History of the World

CHAPTER TWO
DAY OF FIRE

WEDNESDAY, MARCH 26

Not everyone who survived the initial rush of water survived the first night after the flooding. Some people, clinging to rooftops or huddled in attics, froze to death. As the sun rose on Wednesday, high winds increased the threat of fires. Rescuers in boats did what they could to save those in the flood zone. Survivors trapped in buildings made desperate trips across rooftops and window ledges to escape the flames spreading through downtown Dayton.

JOHN BELL

John Bell worked the telephone all night, updating the governor on the disaster unfolding in Dayton. On Wednesday morning, Governor Cox told him he had declared martial law in Dayton. This meant that once the water went down, the streets would be cleared of people and the National Guard would be sent in to help. He also told Bell that relief trains bringing food, water, and bedding were on the way. Finally, someone from the outside was helping.

JOHN PATTERSON

John Patterson stayed up all night leading the rescue efforts. Rescuers steered boats, including those built by Patterson's carpenters, toward the floodwaters. The boats couldn't reach downtown because the water was so deep and swift, but rescuers were able to reach areas on the outskirts of downtown. Thankful survivors were brought to a clearinghouse at the edge of the flood zone, where they signed their names and recorded where they were going so friends and family could find them later. People in automobiles were ready to take survivors to hospitals, schools, and shelters like the one set up at the National Cash Register Company.

By Order of Gov. James M. Cox
The City of Dayton, Ohio
Has been placed under
Martial Law
By his orders I hereby assume command of troops on duty

The citizens of this city are requested to be of service to the National Guard by remaining in their homes, or if out on business remain as far from the flooded district as possible. No sight seers or excursionists will be allowed to disembark in Dayton. The various railroads are requested to assist in the enforcement of this measure by refusing the sale of tickets to others than those having the most urgent business in the City of Dayton.

The strictest sanitary regulations will be enforced and citizens are requested to do their utmost to assist in this regard.

Violators of these orders will be promptly arrested and confined until such time as they can be tried by the proper Military Tribunal. Thieves, Looters and Robbers will be dealt with summarily.

By Order of

Official
John W. Pattison,
Chief of Staff.

Chas. X. Zimerman,
Colonel Fifth Infantry,
Commanding Offic

The declaration of martial law told residents to stay in their homes and to cooperate with the National Guard.

YOUNG RESCUERS

Among the rescuers using boats built by Patterson's carpenters were Patterson's teenage son, Fred, and Fred's best friend, Nelson Talbott. According to John Patterson, they rescued "at least forty women and children." When Patterson urged his son to rest, Fred refused and went back to the floodwaters to search for more people.

Fred Patterson and
Nelson Talbott *(above)*

CLARENCE MAUCH

Upon waking Wednesday morning, Clarence Mauch and the others in the Beckel Building found the surrounding water still high, but it looked as though it might be going down. Then, at quarter past one in the afternoon, they heard an explosion. They rushed up the stairs to the roof to see what had happened. The entire block south of them was burning. Smoke and flames spread quickly, fanned by the wind. The survivors looked at one another, fear in their eyes. This building had protected them from the flood, but they were afraid it wouldn't protect them from the fire. Moving north again was their only option.

Mauch and his group yelled to people in the building to the north. One of the men with Mauch had brought rope from the Patterson Tool Company, a store downtown. It proved to be a good idea. They threw the rope to the people in the next building and stretched it tight against the front of the two outside walls. Mauch stepped out onto a narrow ledge and clutched the rope for safety.

The others followed one at a time, inching across the ledges, careful not to look down. Still holding onto the rope, they stepped across a narrow space to the cornice on the front of the next building and into a window. A much larger group

of people was already in this building. They cheered Mauch and his group as they made it inside.

The group had to keep moving to escape the fires spreading behind them. They tossed a rope to people in the next building and the next. At each building, more survivors joined their journey north. They eventually reached a 12-foot (3.7 m) gap that separated them from the next building. It was too far to cross. Mauch climbed the stairs to the roof to look at the situation. He could see flames whipping in the wind, red-hot embers flying in all directions. Smoke stung his nose and eyes. They needed to keep moving. The others were already busy figuring out what to do.

First, they joined Mauch on the roof. They tied a heavy rope to the chimney and tossed it across the gap to men on the roof of the next building. Those men tied the rope to an iron vent pipe on their roof. A slanting rope line then connected the two buildings. They fashioned a hammock-like rope chair to hang on the slanting rope.

A young boy was the first to climb into the rope chair. He held on tight as he slid across to the next roof. The people in the next building flung the chair back for the others. Some were too nervous to put their weight in the chair and chose instead to cross the space hand over hand, hanging from the rope.

Soon the gap between the buildings was filled with thick smoke. The fire was close behind. Mauch and his group inched across more cornices, climbed down ladders, and walked over shed roofs. After two hours of crawling, swinging, and climbing, they reached a large house. They had finally found shelter from the fires, but people already in the house told them they couldn't stay. Those already inside feared the floors might collapse under the weight of more people. Looking back, Mauch and the others saw the fire still coming toward them.

BILL SLOAN

Bill Sloan continued his rowing and rescuing all day Wednesday. His was one of the few boats on the west side of the river. The west side of Dayton housed many working people, and some neighborhoods were crowded with families. Sloan knew those families needed help, and he couldn't quit.

MARY ALTHOFF

On Wednesday morning, Mary Althoff rushed to the library windows, scared of what she would find. She called out to the boy in the tree. He answered in a weak voice. He was still alive. He had been clinging to the tree for twenty hours.

Boaters travel down Third Street in West Dayton.

Around noon, a rowboat appeared in the waters below. The two men in the boat struggled to keep it upright against the strong current. Althoff and the others yelled to the boaters, pointing them toward the boy. The boaters waved and steered toward the tree. One grabbed the boy's hand while the other gripped the tree to keep the boat steady. The boy untied himself and climbed down into the boat. Turning toward the library building, one rower threw a rope up to someone hanging out the window. They used the rope to pull the boat closer to the building. One of the men leaned out the second-floor window while the people behind him hung on tight to his legs. The water was so high the boy was able to reach the man in the window, and the boy was pulled to safety. The boaters promised to return as soon as possible and sped away.

The boy was blue and shivering all over. He lay on the floor, exhausted. They had no food or water to give him. They wrapped his body with a buffalo hide they took off the wall of the museum. Slowly, his color returned, and he fell asleep.

Survivors used ropes to guide them across channels of floodwater.

CLARENCE MAUCH

Clarence Mauch and his companions stood in the street, trying to decide what to do. The water was lower, but it tore past at great speed and it still was up to their hips. Because they couldn't stay in the crowded house, they decided to brave crossing the street to find another shelter. They waded into the current and tied the end of a long rope to a telephone pole. They watched anxiously as the first of their group battled his way through the swift water, dodging wreckage as it rushed by. Reaching the other side, he tied the rope to another telephone pole. The rope dipped into the water most of the way across the street. One by one, they pulled themselves to the opposite side. "It was quite a struggle," Mauch said, "but we made it safely."

From there, the group waded through water as they went north. They found an empty house with about 3 feet (0.9 m) of water on its first floor. The second floor was dry. Once inside, they removed their cold, wet clothes. "To get the warmth we needed," Mauch said, "six or seven of us piled onto a double bed, laying crossway, covering with a blanket." A volunteer stayed awake to keep an eye on conditions outside.

The man on lookout duty soon yelled that sparks and flaming debris from the fire were falling close by. He worried the debris might reach the roof above them. The men hurried into their wet clothes again—"not a pleasant experience," Mauch remembered, but at least they were ready to leave if they had to. They stayed in the house and tried to sleep, despite the cold and the constant threat of fire.

MARY ALTHOFF

At the library building on Wednesday afternoon, another explosion broke windows in the museum and sent glass flying. As Mary Althoff and the others crowded around one of the broken windows, they saw fire that "spread and raged wildly—burning its way for two blocks to the water's edge." Heavy smoke billowed from the fire. After much discussion, Althoff and the others decided to stay in their stone building, which they hoped would protect them from fire.

Before dark, the boy who had been rescued from the tree insisted on taking the birchbark canoe off the museum wall to go find food. Althoff was shocked at the idea of using a museum piece like that. But as they lowered the canoe out the window, she decided not to protest. They did need food and water, and the boy was able to find some. He was bringing back a box of canned goods and some milk when his boat hit a tree across from the library. Once again, the boy was stuck. Once again, he was rescued by other boaters passing by. He was brought back to the library drenched, exhausted, and freezing. The food was lost in the rescue. Althoff and the others still had nothing to eat or drink.

Despite their fear, hunger, and thirst, they tried to sleep through the night. Althoff later reported that raging fires leaping 50 feet (15 m) into the air made Wednesday night as "light as day."

Rescuers deliver boxes of bread.

CHAPTER THREE

WAITING FOR RESCUE

THURSDAY, MARCH 27

On Thursday morning, the sun briefly shone on Dayton. But within minutes, it disappeared behind storm clouds. Snow and sleet helped put out the fires, but the cold made miserable work for the men in rescue boats. Bending to their task, they continued to paddle down streets. Some were swept into the swift current and crushed against fire hydrants, trees, and houses. Others were frustrated after failed rescues. Rescuers could not always reach those trapped in buildings, so they threw canned salmon, bread, crackers, water, and milk to the survivors.

More than seventy thousand people across the city were stuck in buildings, in trees, and on poles. Throughout Thursday, rescue efforts continued. Rescue boats dotted the water. Late in the day, the promised relief trains chugged in. One pulled seven train cars of food. Others held tents, stoves, and blankets. The goods were quickly loaded into rescue boats, and the volunteers pulled away to make deliveries.

JOHN PATTERSON

Patterson spent most of the day watching rescue boats leave and return with victims. The rest of the time, he patrolled Building No. 10, the headquarters for the rescue efforts. The first two floors were for feeding victims and volunteers. The third floor was the general hospital where nurses and doctors treated the wounded. The upper floors were sleeping quarters, the seventh for men, and the tenth and eleventh for women. Survivors kept busy eating, sleeping on cots, and telling and retelling their survival stories.

John Patterson *(third from right)* watches over rescue efforts.

A Third Street building destroyed by fire

MARY ALTHOFF

Early Thursday morning, Mary Althoff was standing at a window watching the flames outside. She cried out, waking the others. Part of a hardware company at the corner had collapsed, shooting a flare of fire and debris into the sky. As Althoff and the others watched more debris landing on buildings around them, they decided to post a lookout at each window. They spent the rest of the night keeping watch for fire near the building.

JOHN BELL

John Bell announced in a hoarse voice to Governor Cox on Thursday morning that the floodwaters were receding. Men in boats were continuing to rescue survivors.

Bell made it clear to the governor that the crisis wasn't over, saying, "I can see buildings all around me in flames. People running back and forth waving their hands and crying for help, but no one can save them."

CLARENCE MAUCH

Clarence Mauch and his group woke in their second-floor shelter on Thursday morning. They were cold, but their clothes were dry. The water outside was down to about 2 feet (0.6 m). They considered leaving the building since the water was lower. They decided to stay where they were, however, when a National Guard boat came by and warned them of uncovered manholes in the street. The pressure of the water running under the streets had blown most of the covers off. If Mauch and the others decided to leave the building, they risked falling in manholes they couldn't see through the murky water. They stayed where they were all day Thursday.

BILL SLOAN

Bill Sloan continued rowing and rescuing in the west side of Dayton on Thursday. In the distance, he saw several people bobbing up and down in the floodwater. As he drew closer, he realized they were on a raft. Somehow, they had survived the current. He paddled alongside the raft to find five members of the Caleb family. The family had clung to the raft's edges for about forty-eight hours. Their clothes were soaked and their hands were bloody, but they were alive.

One by one, they climbed into the boat. Sloan took them to safety, glad that he had been able to save them after such a long ordeal. By then he had worked more than sixty hours. He had rescued more than three hundred people from the floodwaters of the west side of Dayton.

A survivor climbs a ladder perched on wreckage to enter a home.

CHAPTER FOUR
THE AFTERMATH

Historians estimate more than one thousand lives were lost across the country during the storm and flooding of 1913. More than four hundred people died in Ohio, most of them in Dayton. The disaster cost the state of Ohio $300 million, or about $7 billion in today's money. More than twenty thousand homes were destroyed.

The *Cincinnati Commercial Tribune* reported that "houses were piled on top of one another three, and in one case, four high." Trees protruded through smashed windows, and hundreds of dead horses lay in the streets. Clothing was strung along telephone wires, and mirrors caught in trees twisted and reflected the sunlight and gleaming water.

A survivor turns to cleanup, shoveling the mud out of a building.

"It was a terrible time, after the flood in Dayton—but everyone helped each other. Families opened their homes and shared what they had with those like us, who lost everything. It was a terrible time, but it was a giving time, and we were all stronger afterward."

—Magdalen Toht, fifteen years old

Inside houses were smashed pianos, ruined books, and furniture that had fallen to pieces. Allen Long, who lived in Dayton, found his house contained "enough mud everywhere inside to grow a crop of potatoes in." One woman said, "The mud was up to the knees of the men's rubber boots, all over the first floor, that filthy, gluey mud." People struggled to clear the mess with snow shovels, pans, and pails, pushing mud across carpets and dumping it into the street.

Telephone crews straightened poles and repaired wires. Soon the outside world was once again within reach. The people of Dayton were able to assure family members they were safe or tell of those who were lost.

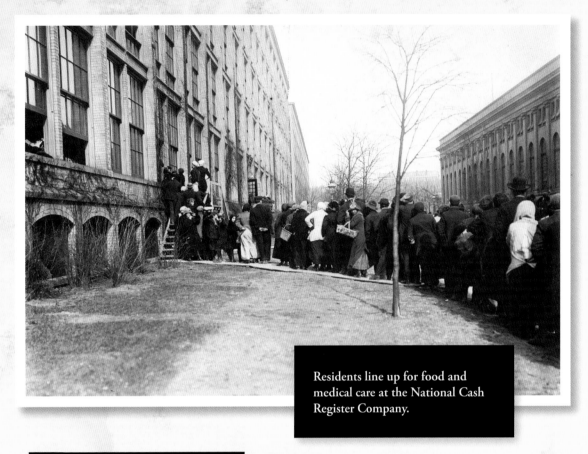

Residents line up for food and medical care at the National Cash Register Company.

JOHN PATTERSON

John H. Patterson was hailed as a national hero. A visitor to Dayton standing in the ruins was asked if he would like to shake hands with Patterson and John Bell. He replied, "Just now I would rather shake hands with those two men than own the National Cash Register Company!"

Fred Patterson and Nelson Talbott remained friends for life. They lived within a few blocks of each other on a hilly part of Dayton. Fred became head of the National Cash Register Company after his father retired.

ANDREW FOX

Andrew "High Water" Fox and his wife returned to their house to clean up. By 1920 he was secretary of the local Young Men's Christian Association (YMCA). The Foxes lived in their repaired house until he died in 1921.

JOHN BELL

John Bell was given a medal by Governor Cox for his heroism during the flood. He remained at his job at the telephone plant in Dayton until World War I (1914–1918), when he managed electrical service at military camps across the United States. After the war, he and his wife moved to Detroit, Michigan. He left the telephone business and went into construction.

CLARENCE MAUCH

Clarence Mauch said, "It was with real pleasure that we stepped into the mud covering the sidewalks and street." To him, Friday, March 28, was "a day of joy for many as thousands of families, who had been separated, were gradually gathered together again."

Mauch and others worked for days to clean up the Finke Company store. Every window was broken, and the store had 2 to 4 feet (0.6 to 1.2 m) of mud that had to be shoveled out. He and his brother, Edward, later started a store of their own in Dayton that sold women's clothing and other items.

Like Mauch and others at the Finke Company, workers at the Delco factory were faced with the difficult task of cleaning out the basement after the flood.

ORVILLE AND KATHARINE WRIGHT

Orville and Katharine Wright hung up signs around Dayton trying to find their father. A friend spotted him sitting on a porch at a home on South Williams Street. Orville and Katharine were reunited with their father. When the Wrights returned to their home on Hawthorn Street, they found the first floor was badly damaged. Later, they discovered that the records, plans, and parts of their original airplane stored on South Williams Street were unharmed.

It took a few weeks for workers at the airplane factory in Dayton to return, but they were soon working again. The Wright business gave money to the city for the cleanup effort. Their collection of documents, including the original plans for their airplane, is stored today at the Smithsonian National Air and Space Museum in Washington, DC.

"And over all, the unheeding sun smiled and smiled again; the first birds of spring twittered and hopped, and the fresh green buds of the trees seemed to swell and grow visibly in the warm soft air. It was a contrast of death in life and life in death such as only a world's tragedy such as this could furnish."

—Cincinnati Commercial Tribune, *unnamed reporter*

BILL SLOAN

Bill Sloan took the pitcher's mound once again. Every time he did, the crowd cheered. He was a hero. For the residents on the west side of the river, he was every bit as much a hero as John Patterson. Sloan died young at the age of forty-one. His tombstone in the Dayton Woodlawn Cemetery reads, "William G. Sloan, 1890–1931. Southpaw Pitcher for the Dayton Marcos, Hero of the 1913 Great Dayton Flood, Saving Over 300 Souls."

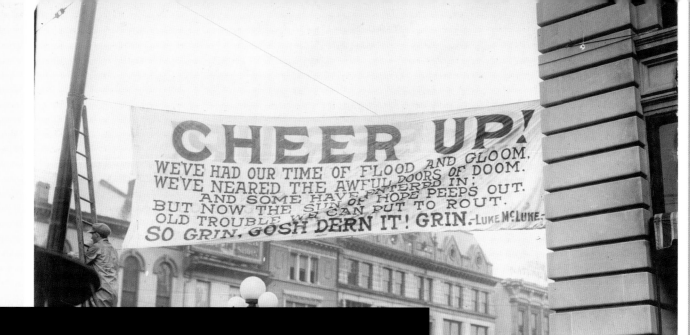

Above: A banner hung in Dayton after the flood reads, "Cheer up! We've had our time of flood and gloom. We've neared the awful doors of doom. And some have entered in; but now the sun of hope peeps out. Old trouble we can put to rout. So grin, gosh dern it! Grin." *Right:* Althoff later typed her account of what happened, noting that "all of this happened more quickly than I can tell it."

MARY ALTHOFF

Mary Althoff climbed into a flimsy boat on Friday after her companions refused to chance it. "Anxiety for my people gave courage," she said. Althoff was taken to her brother's house, where she found out, to her relief, that her family was safe. "Grateful," she said, "we were ready to begin again."

The memories of the flood weighed on Althoff well after 1913. "We were doomed to witness," she said, "and with no power to prevent." She later reported that thoughts of "the days and nights spent in the Library during the Flood of 1913; of the dangers from fire and water and floating wreckage, of the bitter cold and pangs of hunger that we suffered, the exhaustion and anxiety—all crowd back upon me with a sense of oppression difficult to throw off."

Books that could be saved were stacked on tables in the library. A sign on the wall reads, "Silence is the rule of this room."

Once back at work, she and the other library staff found that about forty-five thousand books were soaked with water. Volunteers were able to dry only twenty-five hundred of them. New books arrived from all across the country. Women in Dayton raised money to buy children's books, and the library opened again in June. Althoff worked at the library until she retired in 1932.

LEGENDS OF THE FLOOD

A man near Albany, New York, during the storm reported witnessing his barn whirl away downriver with five horses, three pigs, and hundreds of chickens inside. According to the report, the barn crashed onshore 6 miles (9.7 km) downstream. The terrified horses were found standing with their heads above water. The pigs were balanced on floating wood, and chickens perched safely on the upper rafters. Did this really happen? It is common for dramatic stories to be told after a disaster. Some of these stories are true, and some are greatly exaggerated.

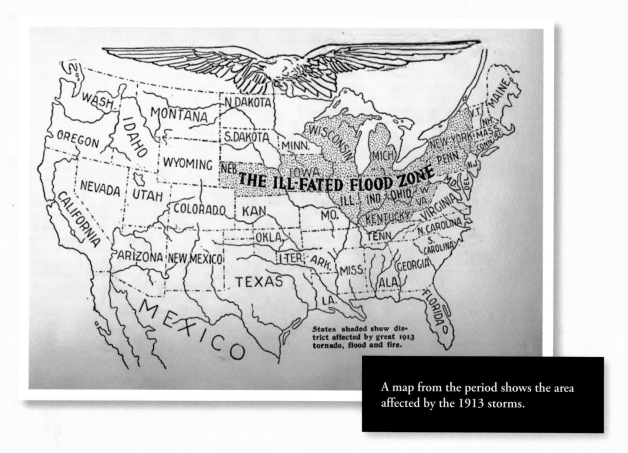

Inside map labels: WASH. MONTANA N.DAKOTA ... WIS. ... VT. N.H. MAINE MASS. CONN. OREGON IDAHO S.DAKOTA MINN. MICH. NEW YORK PENN. N.J. WYOMING NEB. IOWA **THE ILL-FATED FLOOD ZONE** ILL. IND. OHIO W. VA. DEL. MD. NEVADA UTAH CALIFORNIA COLORADO KAN. MO. KENTUCKY VIRGINIA N.CAROLINA ARIZONA NEW MEXICO OKLA. I.TER. ARK. TENN. S. CAROLINA GEORGIA TEXAS MISS. ALA. FLORIDA LA. MEXICO

States shaded show district affected by great 1913 tornado, flood and fire.

A map from the period shows the area affected by the 1913 storms.

THE STORM CONTINUES

After hitting Dayton, the storm spread east into Pennsylvania, New York, New Jersey, and New England. On Tuesday, tornadoes ripped through Pennsylvania. In Altoona, Pennsylvania, tops of railroad cars blew off in the wind and stacks of lumber waiting to be loaded on trains rolled down the street.

New York State suffered the worst flooding it had experienced in 150 years. Rain fell for thirty hours straight. Winds of 60 miles (97 km) per hour hit New York City on Thursday. The cities of Buffalo, Rochester, Albany, and Troy, New York, were hit hard. Wind and snow howled across the state. At the time, the average number of telephone calls per day in Albany was 90,000. On Thursday, March 27, there were 250,000 calls from people looking for help or checking on loved ones. Telephone workers ate and slept in their offices.

The *Dayton Daily News* praises the response of the city's citizens. In a piece below the headline, John Patterson asks for undertakers to report to the National Cash Register Company.

CHAPTER FIVE

RESULTS FROM RUIN

The storm of 1913 was the worst many communities in the Midwest and northeastern states had ever experienced. So why has it been largely forgotten? The *Titanic*, a British passenger ship carrying more than fifteen hundred people, had sunk in the Atlantic the year before the storm. World War I started the year after. The loss of lives and property in this flood faded from the headlines.

But the storm has not been completely forgotten. Many of the procedures used by the city, state, and US government during the flood are still used today to respond to natural disasters. In 1913 it was expected that city and state governments would handle their own emergencies and provide money and people for cleanup.

Despite this, Ohio's Governor Cox called President Woodrow Wilson at the height of the storm to ask for help. Within ten minutes of Cox's appeal, Wilson ordered the War Department to ship tents, food, and medical supplies to the flooded areas. He then called members of Congress and urged them to pass a law allowing the use of War Department supplies. Today FEMA (the Federal Emergency Management Agency) is the arm of the US government that provides aid to communities in disasters across the country.

Governor James M. Cox

After the storm, the city of Dayton made plans to prevent future floods. In 1913 levees were the most common flood control measure in the United States. At the end of the nineteenth century, engineers began building dams and large basins called reservoirs to hold back and collect floodwaters. After the flood, an organization called the Miami Conservancy District was created to build a new flood control system along the Great Miami River. The people of Dayton raised over $2 million to build five dams and reservoirs. Since the 1913 flood, those dams have held back floodwaters from Dayton fifteen hundred times.

In 1913 the American Red Cross was a small organization in Washington, DC. Wilson chose the group to take charge of relief work in Ohio after the flood. Red Cross workers gave food and medical supplies to those in need. The head of the organization at the time, Ernest P. Bicknell, wrote, "This was the largest relief task for which the Red Cross had assumed sole responsibility up to that time."

HURRICANE KATRINA

On August 29, 2005, Hurricane Katrina hit southeastern Louisiana. New Orleans was hit the hardest. Like Dayton, New Orleans became a symbol of the storm. As in Dayton, the flooding was caused by levee failures. In New Orleans, levees failed in over fifty spots, eventually putting 80 percent of New Orleans under water. The total cost of the storm was about $125 billion. More than eighteen hundred lives were lost.

New Orleans residents wade through water that the city's levees failed to hold back after Hurricane Katrina struck on August 29, 2005.

MAJOR FLOODS IN THE UNITED STATES

Flood	Causes	Property damage*	Casualties
Johnstown, Pennsylvania, flood, 1889	Heavy rainfall, broken dam	$425 million	More than 2,000 lives
Great Dayton Flood, 1913	Heavy rainfall, topped levees	$7 billion in Ohio	More than 1,000 lives across the entire storm path
Red River Flood and fires (CAN, ND, and MN), 1997	Heavy snowfall, topped levees	$3.5 billion	0 lives
New Orleans, LA, 2005	Hurricane Katrina, levee failures	$125 billion	More than 1,800 lives

*in 2015 dollars

The Taylorsville Dam on the Great Miami River is one of five dams managed by the Miami Conservancy District.

Although dealing with their own cleanup after the storm, residents of Cleveland, Ohio, used their charity group called the Community Chest to send medical supplies and nurses to Dayton. The Community Chest had been formed only one month before the storm. Its mission was to bring together many charities under one organization. Other Community Chest groups were formed across the United States. They later became the United Way.

Since the 1913 storm, groups such as the Red Cross and United Way have gained experience organizing relief efforts and saving lives. But natural disasters still challenge communities around the world. The efforts of people like Bill Sloan and John Patterson show us how people can help one another during these difficult times.

AUTHOR'S NOTE

I was working in an old factory building for the State of New York when I noticed high-water marks that recorded historic floods on a brick wall. The highest line of all was labeled "1913." When I began researching the 1913 disaster, I quickly realized how widespread it had been. Yet what was known as the Great Dayton Flood is so little known today. I wanted to learn more about the storm and why such a historic flood had been largely forgotten.

I found that historians, librarians, and descendants of those who experienced the storm have not at all forgotten it. I visited the Miami Conservancy District headquarters and the Dayton Metro Library to read firsthand accounts of heroism and survival by people like Mary Althoff and Clarence Mauch. I was struck by how strong these people were in the face of the storm. John Patterson, Bill Sloan, and so many others show us how ordinary people can help others in a disaster.

But how does an author write about people she's never met and an experience she's never had? Primary sources such as newspapers and photos told me what people did during the storm and what they looked like. For details such as Mary Althoff pulling up her long skirts to climb the library steps, I researched clothing of the period. Any thoughts the characters have in this book come from their own accounts or from logical assumptions—that Orville and Katharine would worry for their father, for example.

Yet for all the research, there are things we can't know. For example, we don't know why Bill Sloan threatened Leroy Crandall with a gun. Some sources say Sloan was anxious to rescue his young son trapped somewhere in Dayton, but details are scarce. More significantly, we don't know as much about what people in the poorer neighborhoods experienced during the storm. Nor do we know the experiences of many African Americans other than Sloan. Reporters were more interested in talking to people like John Patterson and Orville Wright than they were in talking to immigrant families and working-class people on the west side of Dayton.

Thankfully, we have the firsthand accounts of survivors that give us an idea of what the world was like at the time of the flood. The people in this story are particular to Dayton, Ohio, in 1913, but their bravery and sense of community continue to inspire anyone who reads their stories.

TIMELINE

March 20–21: High winds roar across the Midwest, and heavy rain raises river and stream levels.

March 22: Most of the Midwest is cut off from the rest of the country with no functioning telephone lines.

March 23: Rain moves to the lower Great Lakes, western New York, and western Pennsylvania throughout the day. Tornadoes form in Michigan, Indiana, Illinois, Iowa, and Nebraska.

March 24: Rain reaches the Atlantic Ocean. The storm system is stalled because a high-pressure system off the Atlantic prevents the rain from going out to sea.

March 25: A wall of water roars down Dayton's streets. Snow falls from New England to Texas. Flooding hits Columbus, Ohio; Pennsylvania; and western New York State.

March 26: New York and New Jersey experience floods up to 12 feet (3.7 m) deep. Only one railroad line works between New York City and Chicago.

March 27: A band of rain is stalled from New York to North Carolina. The rain has turned to snow in the Midwest.

March 28: The storm finally moves out to sea. Water recedes in Dayton, and cleanup begins.

March 29: Cities in Kentucky, Pennsylvania, and New York are still without phone service.

March 30: Water continues to rise in the eastern states. The levee breaks in the Mississippi River as floodwaters from the Ohio River rush in.

March 31: Water continues to rise in Cincinnati, Ohio. Relief boats arrive in Indianapolis, Indiana, where only forty houses remain above water.

April 1: Water levels begin to fall in Cincinnati and Kentucky.

April 3: Smallpox breaks out in a camp of survivors in Kentucky.

April 4: Rain continues in Kentucky, breaking levees.

April 5: New York State is still fighting floods. Indianapolis, Indiana, begins its cleanup.

April 6: Ohio begins its recovery, and the railroad is open for delivery of supplies.

April 8: Floodwaters cause Mississippi River levees to break near Memphis, Tennessee.

SOURCE NOTES

5 Curt Dalton, *Through Flood, through Fire: Personal Stories from Survivors of the Dayton Flood of 1913* (Dayton, OH: printed by author, 2001), 85.

6 Ibid., 9.

15 Ibid., 2.

16 Ibid.

16 Ibid.

18 Ibid., 1.

19 Ibid.

22 Ibid., 2.

23 Dalton, *Through Flood,* available online at http://www .daytonhistorybooks.com/page/page/1645297.htm.

24 Mary Althoff, "The Dayton Library in the Flood, a Personal Record," n.d., Dayton Metro Library, Dayton, OH, 2–3.

25 Dalton, *Through Flood,* http://www.daytonhistorybooks .com/page/page/4583089.htm.

28 Logan Marshall, *The True Story of Our National Calamity of Flood, Fire and Tornado . . . : How the Whole Nation Joined in the Work of Relief.* (Lima, OH: Webb, 1913), 49.

32 Dalton, *Through Flood,* 2.

32 Ibid.

33 Dalton, *Through Flood,* http://www.daytonhistorybooks .com/page/page/4583089.htm.

33 Althoff, "The Dayton Library," 3.

33 Ibid.

37 Dalton, *Through Flood,* http://www.daytonhistorybooks .com/page/page/1645346.htm.

38 Dalton, *Through Flood,* 76.

39 Marshall, *The True Story,* 21.

39 Dalton, *Through Flood,* 46.

39 Ibid.

40 Dalton, *Through Flood,* http://www.daytonhistorybooks .com/page/page/1645346.htm.

41 Dalton, *Through Flood,* available online http://www .daytonhistorybooks.com/page/page/4583089.htm.

41 Ibid.

42 Dalton, *Through Flood,* 85.

42 "William G. Sloan," Find a Grave, August 2, 2013, http://www.findagrave.com/cgi-bin/fg.cgi?page=pv&G Rid=114783265&PIpi=85619601.

43 Althoff, "The Dayton Library," 17.

43 Ibid., 4.

43 Ibid., 1.

47 Dalton, *Through Flood,* http://www.daytonhistorybooks .com/page/page/4512697.htm.

GLOSSARY

birchbark canoe: a type of canoe traditionally used by some Native American groups

cornice: a ledge on the outside of a building

dam: a structure built across a river to hold back water

debris: pieces of something that has been broken

foundry: a factory for melting and shaping metal

horse and buggy: a carriage pulled by a horse

infirmary: a place where sick people are cared for

lantern: a kind of lamp with glass sides that burns oil or gas for light

National Guard: members of the military who are available on reserve

reins: straps attached to the bridle that fits around a horse's head

saturate: to soak thoroughly

streetcar: a vehicle carrying many people that runs on electricity

surge: a sudden, strong rush

telegraph: a device that sent messages over long distances using code, in use in the United States until telephone service replaced the telegraph in the early twentieth century

tributary: a stream that flows into a river or lake

undertaker: a person who prepares a body for burial or cremation

War Department: the government department that controlled the operation of the US Army from 1798 until 1947

SELECTED BIBLIOGRAPHY

Bell, Trudy E. *The Great Dayton Flood of 1913*. Charleston, SC: Arcadia, 2008.

Dalton, Curt. *Through Flood, through Fire: Personal Stories from Survivors of the Dayton Flood of 1913*. Dayton, OH: printed by author, 2001. Also available online at http://www.daytonhistorybooks.com/page/page/1644414.htm.

Eckert, Allan W. *A Time of Terror: The Great Dayton Flood*. Dayton, OH: Landfall, 1965.

Macfarlane, Peter Clark. "In Stricken Dayton: A Star Reporter's Vivid Story of the Misery and Heroism in a City Distressed by Fire and Flood." *Collier's* 51, no. 4 (April 12, 1913): 8–9.

Marshall, Logan. *The True Story of Our National Calamity of Flood, Fire and Tornado . . . : How the Whole Nation Joined in the Work of Relief*. Lima, OH: Webb, 1913.

PLACES TO VISIT

Carillon Historical Park
　　1000 Carillon Blvd.
　　Dayton, OH 45409
　　http://www.daytonhistory.org/
　　This museum, dedicated to Dayton history, houses the original 1905 Wright Flyer III airplane designed by the Wright brothers, along with a collection of cash registers produced by Patterson's National Cash Register Company.

Patterson Homestead
　　1815 Brown St.
　　Dayton, OH 45409
　　http://www.daytonhistory.org/destinations/patterson-homestead-2/
　　The historic Patterson house occupied by the family from 1804 to 1904 includes a gallery devoted to the story of Patterson's company.

The Wright Family Home
　　7 Hawthorn St.
　　Dayton, OH 45402
　　http://airandspace.si.edu/exhibitions/wright-brothers/online/who/1884/family.cfm
　　This site of the Wright family home at the time of the 1913 flood is open to visitors, while the Wright house itself was moved to Dearborn, Michigan, and is also open to the public.

FOR MORE INFORMATION

Books

Brown, Don. *Drowned City: Hurricane Katrina and New Orleans*. New York: Houghton Mifflin Harcourt, 2014. See how the flooding of New Orleans unfolded in these illustrated stories of Hurricane Katrina.

Marquardt, Meg. *The Science of a Flood*. Ann Arbor, MI: Cherry Lake, 2016. Read about historic floods, what causes them, and how scientists try to predict them.

Old, Wendie. *The Wright Brothers: Aviation Pioneers and Inventors*. Berkeley Heights, NJ: Enslow, 2015. Learn more about the lives of the Wright brothers and their historic first flight in Kitty Hawk, North Carolina.

Websites

Flood of 1913 Photos
　　http://www.daytondailynews.com/gallery/news/flood-1913-photos/g5bR/#2738149
　　Browse photos of the 1913 flood collected by the *Dayton Daily News*.

The Great Dayton Flood of 1913
　　http://www.daytonhistorybooks.com/page/page/1566099.htm
　　Read personal histories of those who survived the flood.

INDEX

PHOTO ACKNOWLEDGMENTS

The images in this book are used with the permission of: © pashabo/Shutterstock.com (frame); © Ortis/Shutterstock.com (stained paper background); © Valentin Agapov/Shutterstock.com (paper stack); Library of Congress pp. 4 (LC-DIG-det-4a12175); 17 (LC-DIG-ppmsca-17310); 26 (LC-DIG-pga-03904); Dayton Metro Library, pp. 6, 7, 9 (top), 12 (bottom), 15, 18 (bottom), 19, 21 (all), 22, 23, 28 (right), 29, 31, 34, 35, 36, 38, 39, 40, 41, 43 (all), 44 (top), 46, 50–51, 52–53, 54–55, 56, and all newspaper backgrounds; © Laura Westlund/Independent Picture Service, pp. 8–9; © Bettman/Corbis, p. 9 (middle); © Ohio Historical Society, pp. 9 (bottom), 10, 18 (top), 27, 47; © Everett Collection Inc./Alamy, p. 11; © Dorling Kindersley/Getty Images, p. 13; © Special Collections and Archives, Wright State University Libraries, p. 14; via http://www.daytonflood.net, p. 20; Courtesy of Trudy E. Bell Collection from page 67 of *Rasende Fluten und Tobende Stür* by Thomas H. Russel, p. 45; © Chris Graythen/Getty Images, p. 48.

Front cover: Dayton Metro Library; © pashabo/Shutterstock.com (frame).

Back cover and jacket flaps: Dayton Metro Library; © Ortis/Shutterstock.com (stained paper).